Operation Northwoods: The U.S. Military Intervention in Cuba that Never Happened

Copyright Page

TITLE: Operation Northwoods: The U.S. Military Intervention in Cuba that Never Happened

1ST Edition

Table of Contents

Operation Northwoods: The U.S. Military Intervention in Cuba that Never Happened

By Roberto Miguel Rodriguez

Chapter 1: Operation Northwoods: The 1962 U.S. project for military intervention in Cuba that never happened

Historical context: U.S.-Cuba relations leading up to Operation Northwoods

The subchapter "Historical context: U.S.-Cuba relations leading up to Operation Northwoods" provides crucial background information for understanding the events that led to the controversial military project. In order to fully grasp the significance and implications of Operation Northwoods, it is essential to explore the historical dynamics between the United States and Cuba.

Throughout the 20th century, U.S.-Cuba relations had been marked by a complex interplay of political, economic, and ideological factors. Following the Spanish-American War of 1898, the United States emerged as a dominant power in Cuba, exerting significant influence over its affairs. This influence reached its peak during the Cold War era, as the United States sought to contain the spread of communism.

The Cuban Revolution in 1959, led by Fidel Castro, dramatically altered the U.S.-Cuba relationship. Castro's socialist policies and alignment with the Soviet Union posed a direct challenge to U.S. interests in the region. In response, the United States implemented a series of economic sanctions and covert operations aimed at destabilizing the Castro regime.

Operation Northwoods, conceived in 1962, emerged as part of this broader context. It was within the framework of heightened tensions and a desire to undermine the Castro government that the project was proposed. Operation Northwoods aimed to create a pretext for military intervention in Cuba, employing deceptive and provocative tactics such as staged terrorist attacks on U.S. soil, hijackings, and the shooting down of civilian aircraft.

The decision-making process behind Operation Northwoods was influenced by a range of factors, including the political climate of the time and the perceived threat of communism. However, the project faced significant opposition from within the Kennedy administration, particularly from top military officials who deemed it too extreme and morally objectionable.

The declassification of Operation Northwoods documents in recent years has sparked widespread interest and debate among historians. The revelation of such a controversial project has led to further examination of the role of intelligence agencies and the military-industrial complex in planning and executing covert operations.

Moreover, Operation Northwoods has had a lasting impact on U.S.-Cuba relations and the formulation of future military strategies. The project serves as a cautionary tale, raising questions about the ethical boundaries of intelligence operations and the manipulation of public opinion through psychological warfare and propaganda tactics.

The international response to the declassified Operation Northwoods documents has also been significant. The revelations have fueled conspiracy theories and further strained U.S. relations with Cuba and other nations. The declassification has prompted calls for greater transparency and accountability in the conduct of covert operations.

In conclusion, exploring the historical context of U.S.-Cuba relations leading up to Operation Northwoods provides critical insights into the motivations, decision-making, and ramifications of this controversial military project. By delving into this historical analysis, historians can gain a deeper understanding of the factors that shaped U.S. foreign policy and military strategies during the Cold War era.

Overview of Operation Northwoods: Objectives and proposed military actions

Operation Northwoods was a controversial and secretive project conceived by the U.S. Department of Defense and Joint Chiefs of Staff in 1962. Its primary objective was to create a pretext for military intervention in Cuba by orchestrating a series of false flag attacks and acts of terrorism, all to be blamed on the Cuban government. This subchapter aims to provide a comprehensive overview of the objectives and proposed military actions of Operation Northwoods, shedding light on the historical impact it has had on U.S.-Cuba relations.

The objectives of Operation Northwoods were multifold. Firstly, it aimed to justify a full-scale invasion of Cuba, which was seen as a threat to American interests during the Cold War era. Secondly, the operation sought to garner public support for such an invasion by manipulating public opinion through psychological warfare and propaganda tactics. Moreover, it aimed to create a pretext for international intervention, using fabricated evidence to convince other nations of the need for military action against Cuba.

To achieve these objectives, a range of military actions were proposed under Operation Northwoods. These included hijacking American civilian aircraft and blaming it on Cuban forces, orchestrating terrorist attacks on U.S. soil and blaming them on Cuban agents, and conducting covert military operations disguised as Cuban forces attacking U.S. military installations. These proposed actions were designed to create a sense of urgency and fear among the American public, thereby justifying military intervention.

The subchapter will delve into the decision-making process behind Operation Northwoods, analyzing the role of the military-industrial complex and intelligence agencies in planning and executing such covert operations. It will also draw comparisons between Operation

Northwoods and other covert operations in U.S. history, highlighting the unique aspects and controversies surrounding this particular project.

Furthermore, the subchapter will explore the political ramifications of Operation Northwoods and the controversies it generated. It will examine the impact of the operation on U.S.-Cuba relations, as well as its legacy in shaping future military strategies. Additionally, it will discuss the international response to the declassification of Operation Northwoods documents, shedding light on the global perception of this clandestine project.

Overall, this subchapter will provide historians with a comprehensive overview of Operation Northwoods, its objectives, proposed military actions, and its historical impact on U.S.-Cuba relations. By delving into the political ramifications, controversies, and decision-making processes behind this covert operation, it will contribute to a deeper understanding of the complex dynamics of U.S. foreign policy during the Cold War era.

Key players in the planning and development of Operation Northwoods

Operation Northwoods stands as a significant event in the history of U.S.-Cuba relations, a project that was never implemented but carries immense political ramifications and controversies to this day. In this subchapter, we delve into the key players who were involved in the planning and development of this covert operation.

One of the central figures in Operation Northwoods was General Lyman Lemnitzer, the Chairman of the Joint Chiefs of Staff at the time. Lemnitzer played a pivotal role in devising the military intervention plan, which aimed to justify U.S. military involvement in Cuba through a series of false flag attacks and acts of terrorism. His influence, as the highest-ranking military officer, cannot be underestimated in the decision-making process behind Operation Northwoods.

Another key player was Brigadier General Edward Lansdale, a renowned expert in psychological warfare and unconventional tactics. Lansdale's involvement in Operation Northwoods reflected the emphasis on psychological warfare and propaganda tactics proposed in the plan. His expertise in manipulating public opinion and manufacturing consent played a crucial role in the development of Operation Northwoods.

Within the intelligence community, Admiral Arleigh Burke, the Chief of Naval Operations, and General Earle Wheeler, the Director of the Joint Staff, were instrumental in shaping the covert operation. Their roles in planning and executing covert operations like Operation Northwoods highlight the involvement of intelligence agencies in such endeavors.

The military-industrial complex also had a significant stake in Operation Northwoods. Defense contractors and high-ranking officials within the defense industry had a vested interest in promoting military interventions and bolstering defense spending. Their influence on the planning and development of Operation Northwoods cannot be overlooked.

Moreover, political figures such as President John F. Kennedy and Secretary of Defense Robert McNamara were aware of Operation Northwoods, although their exact roles in the project remain a subject of debate among historians. The declassification of Operation Northwoods documents sparked an international response, shedding light on the covert operations conducted by the U.S. government and raising questions about the ethics and legality of such endeavors.

Understanding the key players involved in Operation Northwoods is essential for a comprehensive historical analysis of the decision-making process behind the project. Their roles, motivations, and influence shed light on the legacy of Operation Northwoods and its impact on future military strategies. As historians, it is crucial to examine not only the events themselves but also the individuals and institutions behind them to gain a deeper understanding of the complexities at play.

The Kennedy administration's response to Operation Northwoods

The Kennedy administration's response to Operation Northwoods was a pivotal moment in U.S. history that showcased the president's commitment to ethical leadership and transparency in government. Operation Northwoods, a top-secret plan proposed in 1962, aimed to create a pretext for military intervention in Cuba by orchestrating a series of false flag attacks and acts of terrorism on U.S. soil. However, President John F. Kennedy, upon learning about the plan, promptly rejected it and ordered its immediate termination.

Kennedy's decision to reject Operation Northwoods was driven by several factors. Firstly, he recognized the potential political ramifications and controversies that would arise if the plan were to be executed. The use of deceptive tactics and the potential loss of innocent lives would have undoubtedly sparked outrage among the American public and the international community. Kennedy understood that such actions would undermine the credibility and moral authority of the United States.

Moreover, the president's historical analysis of the decision-making process behind Operation Northwoods shed light on the dangerous influence of the military-industrial complex. This plan, devised by high-ranking military officials and intelligence agencies, exemplified the alarming collusion between the defense industry and the government. Kennedy recognized the need to maintain civilian control over the military and prevent the unchecked power of the military-industrial complex from compromising the nation's values and interests.

The Kennedy administration's response to Operation Northwoods also played a significant role in shaping future military strategies. By rejecting this covert operation, Kennedy established a precedent that emphasized the importance of open dialogue, diplomatic negotiations, and peaceful resolutions to conflicts. This legacy influenced subsequent administrations and paved the way for alternative approaches to international relations, contributing to a shift away from aggressive military interventions.

Furthermore, the declassification of Operation Northwoods documents sparked international response and shed light on the role of intelligence agencies in planning and executing covert operations. Historians and researchers delved into the psychological warfare and propaganda tactics proposed in Operation Northwoods, revealing the extent to which intelligence agencies were willing to manipulate public opinion and orchestrate false narratives to further their objectives.

In conclusion, the Kennedy administration's response to Operation Northwoods remains a significant chapter in U.S. history. By rejecting this covert plan, Kennedy demonstrated his commitment to ethical leadership, transparency, and the preservation of democratic values. The impact of Operation Northwoods on U.S.-Cuba relations, the role of the military-industrial complex, and the global response to its declassification have all contributed to a deeper understanding of the complexities and challenges associated with covert operations and their implications for international relations.

Reasons for the eventual abandonment of Operation Northwoods

Operation Northwoods, the classified U.S. project for military intervention in Cuba, was a controversial plan that ultimately never came to fruition. The reasons for its eventual abandonment were varied and complex, reflecting a combination of political, strategic, and ethical considerations.

One key reason for the abandonment of Operation Northwoods was the political ramifications and controversies surrounding the plan. When the details of the operation were revealed, it sparked public outrage and raised serious concerns about the United States' moral standing. The plan involved false flag operations and acts of terrorism that could have resulted in civilian casualties, which went against the principles of democracy and human rights that the U.S. claimed to uphold. The potential backlash from both domestic and international communities made it increasingly difficult for the government to justify the operation.

Furthermore, the decision-making process behind Operation Northwoods underwent historical analysis, which revealed flaws and inconsistencies. As the plan was scrutinized by policymakers and military officials, doubts arose regarding its feasibility and potential effectiveness. Questions were raised about the reliability of intelligence reports, the level of support from allies, and the long-term implications of such a covert operation. These uncertainties ultimately led to the conclusion that Operation Northwoods was not a viable strategy for achieving U.S. objectives in Cuba.

Another significant factor in the abandonment of Operation Northwoods was the role of the military-industrial complex. While the plan was initially proposed by the Joint Chiefs of Staff, it faced resistance from within the military establishment itself. Some military leaders expressed concerns about the long-term consequences of initiating such a risky operation. This internal opposition, combined with the growing anti-war sentiment among the general public, contributed to the decision to abandon the operation.

The comparison between Operation Northwoods and other covert operations in U.S. history also shed light on the potential risks and negative consequences associated with such endeavors. The lessons learned from past operations, such as the Iran-Contra affair or the Bay of Pigs invasion, demonstrated the potential for political and strategic failures. These historical parallels further reinforced the decision to abandon Operation Northwoods.

In conclusion, the eventual abandonment of Operation Northwoods can be attributed to a combination of political ramifications and controversies, historical analysis of the decision-making process, the role of the military-industrial complex, and the comparison with other covert operations. These factors contributed to the understanding that the risks and potential fallout outweighed any potential benefits that the operation might have provided. Ultimately, Operation Northwoods remains a cautionary tale in the annals of U.S. history, reminding us of the ethical and strategic considerations that shape military strategies and the delicate balance between national security and democratic values.

Chapter 2: Conspiracy theories surrounding Operation Northwoods

Origins and propagation of conspiracy theories regarding Operation Northwoods

In the realm of covert operations and political intrigue, few events have captured the imagination and spawned as many conspiracy theories as Operation Northwoods. This subchapter aims to delve into the origins and propagation of these theories, shedding light on the various narratives that have emerged surrounding this infamous project.

Operation Northwoods, the 1962 U.S. project for military intervention in Cuba that was never implemented, was a highly classified plan devised by the U.S. Department of Defense. The goal was to justify an invasion of Cuba by staging false flag attacks on American soil, creating a pretext for military action. However, the plan was ultimately rejected by President John F. Kennedy and remained classified until its declassification in the early 2000s.

The existence of Operation Northwoods, once revealed, sparked widespread public interest and speculation. Conspiracy theories emerged, suggesting that the U.S. government had orchestrated or allowed the 1962 Cuban Missile Crisis as a means to justify military intervention. These theories speculated that the Kennedy administration was willing to sacrifice American lives to further its political agenda.

The propagation of these conspiracy theories can be attributed to several factors. Firstly, the secrecy surrounding Operation Northwoods and its subsequent declassification created a fertile ground for speculation. Historians and researchers, hungry for information, sought to fill the gaps in the historical narrative, often resorting to conjecture and supposition.

Secondly, the political ramifications and controversies of Operation Northwoods, combined with existing public distrust of the government, fueled the conspiracy theories. The project's audacious nature, proposing the use of psychological warfare and propaganda tactics, played into the narrative of a shadowy government capable of orchestrating elaborate schemes.

Furthermore, comparisons between Operation Northwoods and other covert operations in U.S. history, such as the Gulf of Tonkin incident and the alleged weapons of mass destruction in Iraq, further contributed to the propagation of conspiracy theories. Skeptics argued that Northwoods was not an isolated incident but rather part of a larger pattern of government deception and manipulation.

While the origins of these conspiracy theories are rooted in speculation and skepticism, it is crucial to approach them with a critical eye. Historical analysis of the decision-making process behind Operation Northwoods reveals complex political dynamics and the interplay between military and intelligence agencies. It is essential to examine the evidence, consider multiple perspectives, and understand the socio-political context in which these theories arise.

In conclusion, the propagation of conspiracy theories surrounding Operation Northwoods can be attributed to the secrecy and controversy surrounding the project, as well as broader public distrust of the government. However, it is important for historians to approach these theories with caution, conducting rigorous research and analysis to separate fact from fiction. By unraveling the origins and narratives surrounding these theories, a more nuanced understanding of Operation Northwoods and its historical impact can be achieved.

Examination of popular conspiracy theories and their impact

One of the most intriguing chapters in the history of U.S.-Cuba relations is undoubtedly Operation Northwoods, the 1962 project for military intervention in Cuba that was never implemented. However, the mere existence of this operation has given rise to numerous conspiracy theories, which have had a significant impact on public perception and historical analysis. In this subchapter, we will delve into these theories and explore their implications.

Conspiracy theories surrounding Operation Northwoods have proliferated over the years, suggesting that the U.S. government was willing to orchestrate false flag operations, including acts of terrorism, to justify a military intervention in Cuba. While these theories remain highly contested, they have undoubtedly shaped public opinion and fueled skepticism towards government actions and motives.

The political ramifications and controversies of Operation Northwoods are equally significant. The decision-making process behind the operation raises questions about the accountability and transparency of government institutions. By examining the historical context and the individuals involved, historians can shed light on the complex dynamics that influenced this covert operation.

Moreover, it is essential to analyze the role of the military-industrial complex in planning Operation Northwoods. This operation provides a window into the relationship between defense contractors, military leaders, and policymakers. Comparisons between Operation Northwoods and other covert operations in U.S. history can highlight patterns and recurring themes, shedding light on the broader strategies employed by the U.S. government.

The impact of Operation Northwoods on U.S.-Cuba relations cannot be understated. While the operation was never implemented, its existence further strained the already fragile relationship between the two nations. Understanding this impact is crucial for comprehending the subsequent developments in U.S.-Cuba relations and the lasting effects of Operation Northwoods on future military strategies.

Psychological warfare and propaganda tactics proposed in Operation Northwoods provide insights into the mindset of intelligence agencies and their modus operandi. By exploring these tactics, historians can gain a deeper understanding of the methods employed by intelligence agencies in planning and executing covert operations like Operation Northwoods.

Furthermore, the international response to the declassification of Operation Northwoods documents is worth investigating. The revelation of this operation had reverberations across the globe, with implications for diplomatic relations and public trust in government actions.

In conclusion, the examination of popular conspiracy theories surrounding Operation Northwoods is vital for historians and scholars alike. By delving into the political, historical, and psychological aspects of this operation, we can gain a comprehensive understanding of its impact on U.S.-Cuba relations, the military-industrial complex, and the broader landscape of covert operations in U.S. history.

Debunking and refuting conspiracy theories surrounding Operation Northwoods

Operation Northwoods, the infamous 1962 U.S. project for military intervention in Cuba that was never implemented, has sparked numerous conspiracy theories since its declassification. However, a closer examination reveals that many of these theories lack substantial evidence and fail to withstand historical scrutiny. This subchapter aims to debunk and refute some of the most prevalent conspiracy theories surrounding Operation Northwoods.

One common conspiracy theory suggests that Operation Northwoods was a false flag operation orchestrated by the U.S. government to create a pretext for invading Cuba. However, extensive historical analysis of the decision-making process behind Operation Northwoods reveals that it was a proposal developed within the military establishment, rather than a top-down government directive. The plan was ultimately rejected by President Kennedy and his administration, demonstrating that it never had the official approval required for implementation.

Another conspiracy theory suggests that Operation Northwoods was part of a broader plan by the military-industrial complex to profit from war. While it is true that some military contractors may have stood to gain financially from a military intervention in Cuba, there is no evidence to suggest that they played a significant role in planning Operation Northwoods. In fact, the rejection of the plan by President Kennedy indicates that the military-industrial complex did not have the power to manipulate government decision-making in this case.

Comparisons between Operation Northwoods and other covert operations in U.S. history have also fueled conspiracy theories. However, it is important to note that Operation Northwoods was an exceptional case. Unlike other covert operations, it was not executed, and its declassification provided valuable insights into the decision-making process and the limits of government approval for such plans.

The impact of Operation Northwoods on U.S.-Cuba relations cannot be overstated. The proposed plan, which included acts of terrorism on U.S. soil, had the potential to severely damage diplomatic relations between the two countries. However, the fact that it was rejected demonstrates a commitment to maintaining peaceful relations and upholding democratic values.

In conclusion, while conspiracy theories surrounding Operation Northwoods may persist, a careful analysis of the historical evidence reveals that they lack credibility. This subchapter aims to provide historians with a comprehensive debunking and refutation of these theories, shedding light on the true nature and political ramifications of Operation Northwoods. By addressing these misconceptions, we can gain a more accurate understanding of this pivotal event in U.S.-Cuba relations and its lasting impact on military strategies and international perceptions.

The role of conspiracy theories in shaping public perception and historical narratives

Conspiracy theories have long played a significant role in shaping public perception and historical narratives, and the case of Operation Northwoods is no exception. Operation Northwoods, the 1962 U.S. project for military intervention in Cuba that was never implemented, has been surrounded by countless conspiracy theories since its declassification. These theories have had a profound impact on how historians view this pivotal event in U.S.-Cuba relations.

One of the main conspiracy theories surrounding Operation Northwoods suggests that it was a false flag operation designed to justify a full-scale invasion of Cuba. Proponents of this theory argue that the U.S. government, particularly the military-industrial complex, sought to create a pretext for military intervention by orchestrating acts of terrorism and blaming them on Cuba. This theory raises questions about the decision-making process behind Operation Northwoods and the potential political ramifications and controversies it would have caused if implemented.

Historical analysis of Operation Northwoods reveals a complex web of factors that influenced the decision-making process. The role of the military-industrial complex cannot be overlooked, as it is widely believed that defense contractors and arms manufacturers played a significant role in planning this operation. Comparisons between Operation Northwoods and other covert operations in U.S. history, such as the Gulf of Tonkin incident and the Iraq War, shed light on the broader strategies employed by the U.S. government.

The impact of Operation Northwoods on U.S.-Cuba relations cannot be underestimated. The revelation of this covert operation has fueled anti-American sentiment in Cuba and has been used by the Cuban government to justify its own actions against the United States. Furthermore, the legacy of Operation Northwoods has had far-reaching consequences in shaping future military strategies, particularly in terms of psychological warfare and propaganda tactics.

The role of intelligence agencies in planning and executing covert operations like Operation Northwoods is a subject of intense scrutiny. The declassification of Operation Northwoods documents has led to increased international attention and a reevaluation of the actions taken by intelligence agencies. The international response to these documents has been mixed, with some countries expressing outrage at the U.S. government's actions, while others see it as a necessary evil in the pursuit of national security.

In conclusion, conspiracy theories surrounding Operation Northwoods have played a significant role in shaping public perception and historical narratives. The impact of these theories on historians cannot be ignored, as they raise important questions about the decision-making process, the role of the military-industrial complex, and the broader strategies employed by the U.S. government. The declassification of Operation Northwoods documents has sparked international debate and has forced a reevaluation of intelligence agencies' actions. As historians, it is crucial to critically analyze these conspiracy theories and their potential implications for our understanding of this pivotal moment in history.

Chapter 3: Political ramifications and controversies of Operation Northwoods

Congressional and public reactions to the declassification of Operation Northwoods documents

The declassification of Operation Northwoods documents in recent years has sparked significant interest and strong reactions from both the public and members of Congress. This subchapter aims to explore the various responses to the release of these classified documents, shedding light on the historical impact of this controversial operation.

For historians studying Operation Northwoods, the declassification of these documents represents a valuable opportunity to delve into the decision-making process that led to the proposal of this covert operation. It allows for a more comprehensive understanding of the political ramifications and controversies surrounding Operation Northwoods. By analyzing the role of the military-industrial complex in planning this operation, historians can draw comparisons between Northwoods and other covert operations in U.S. history, contributing to a broader understanding of U.S. foreign policy.

The impact of Operation Northwoods on U.S.-Cuba relations cannot be underestimated. The declassification of these documents has provided historians with a deeper insight into the strategies employed during the Cold War era. By examining the legacy of Operation Northwoods, historians can explore how this operation shaped future military strategies, particularly in terms of psychological warfare and propaganda tactics proposed.

The response from Congress and the public to the declassification of Operation Northwoods documents has been mixed. Some members of Congress have called for further investigation into the extent of covert operations during this period, while others have expressed concern over the ethical implications of such proposals. The declassification has also fueled conspiracy theories surrounding Operation Northwoods, with some suggesting that similar covert operations may have been executed in the past.

Internationally, the release of these documents has sparked both curiosity and concern. The role of intelligence agencies in planning and executing covert operations like Operation Northwoods has come under scrutiny, leading to debates about the ethics of such actions. The international response to the declassification has further highlighted the delicate nature of intelligence operations and their potential impact on global relations.

In conclusion, the declassification of Operation Northwoods documents has had a profound impact on historians and various niches interested in this topic. It has provided valuable insights into the decision-making process, political ramifications, and controversies surrounding this covert operation. The response from Congress, the public, and the international community has underscored the importance of understanding the role of intelligence agencies and the potential consequences of such covert operations. Operation Northwoods remains a significant historical event that continues to shape our understanding of U.S.-Cuba relations and military strategies.

Impact on domestic politics and public trust in government

The revelation of Operation Northwoods and its declassification documents had a profound impact on domestic politics and public trust in the U.S. government. This subchapter explores the far-reaching consequences that this covert operation had on the nation's political landscape and the erosion of public trust in the government.

One of the immediate political ramifications of Operation Northwoods was the widespread controversy it generated. The American public, upon learning about the government's plans to orchestrate terrorist attacks on its own citizens, was shocked and outraged. This revelation exposed a dark underbelly of the U.S. government's decision-making process and raised serious questions about the ethics and integrity of those in power.

The controversy surrounding Operation Northwoods also gave rise to a surge in conspiracy theories. Skeptics began to question the official narratives and suggested that the government's involvement in covert operations extended far beyond what was disclosed. This skepticism further fueled public mistrust, as citizens became increasingly skeptical of the government's ability to act in their best interests.

The impact on domestic politics was significant. Operation Northwoods sparked a widespread debate on the role of the military-industrial complex in shaping national security strategies. Many historians argue that this clandestine operation exemplified the dangerous influence of the military-industrial complex in planning military interventions. The revelation of Operation Northwoods led to a reevaluation of the decision-making process and a push for greater transparency and accountability in the government.

Furthermore, Operation Northwoods had lasting implications for U.S.-Cuba relations. The declassification of these documents shed light on the extent to which the U.S. government was willing to go in its efforts to undermine the Cuban government. This revelation strained diplomatic ties between the two nations and reinforced the perception of the U.S. as an aggressor in the eyes of the international community.

The legacy of Operation Northwoods in shaping future military strategies cannot be understated. This covert operation highlighted the potential dangers of psychological warfare and propaganda tactics. It served as a cautionary tale for future military planners and led to a reevaluation of the ethical boundaries of covert operations.

In conclusion, Operation Northwoods had far-reaching consequences on domestic politics and public trust in the government. The controversy and conspiracy theories surrounding this operation reshaped the national dialogue on military interventions and exposed the dangerous influence of the military-industrial complex. The impact on U.S.-Cuba relations and the legacy of Operation Northwoods in shaping future military strategies further underscore the significance of this covert operation. The declassification of Operation Northwoods documents triggered a fundamental reevaluation of the government's decision-making process and raised important questions about the balance between national security and public trust.

Ethical implications of planning covert operations against foreign nations

Covert operations have long been a controversial aspect of international relations, raising significant ethical implications. This subchapter delves into the ethical considerations surrounding the planning of covert operations against foreign nations, with a particular focus on Operation Northwoods.

Operation Northwoods, a classified project proposed by the U.S. government in 1962, aimed to justify military intervention in Cuba through a series of false flag operations. The project, although never implemented, has been a subject of conspiracy theories and intense scrutiny. Historians have grappled with the ethical implications of such covert operations, questioning the morality and legality of deceiving the American people and potentially endangering innocent lives.

One of the key ethical dilemmas is the deception of the public. Covert operations inherently involve secrecy and manipulation, leading to a breach of trust between the government and its citizens. Historians must critically analyze the political ramifications and controversies surrounding Operation Northwoods, exploring the extent to which democratic principles were compromised in pursuit of geopolitical interests.

Additionally, the decision-making process behind Operation Northwoods warrants historical analysis. Understanding the motivations and justifications for planning covert operations against foreign nations sheds light on the moral compass of those involved. This subchapter should explore the role of the military-industrial complex in shaping such strategies, examining the influence of defense contractors and their vested interests in maintaining a state of perpetual warfare.

Comparisons with other covert operations in U.S. history provide a broader context for understanding the ethical implications of Operation Northwoods. This subchapter should explore the legacy of Operation Northwoods in shaping future military strategies and the psychological warfare and propaganda tactics proposed in the project. Moreover, it should delve into the role of intelligence agencies in planning and executing covert operations, highlighting the delicate balance between national security and ethical considerations.

Finally, the international response to the declassification of Operation Northwoods documents is crucial in assessing its impact. The revelations surrounding this covert operation have undoubtedly influenced global perceptions of U.S. foreign policy. Historians must examine the ethical implications from a broader perspective, considering the consequences for diplomatic relations and international trust in the United States.

In conclusion, the ethical implications of planning covert operations against foreign nations, as exemplified by Operation Northwoods, demand thorough examination. This subchapter provides historians with a comprehensive analysis of the ethical considerations surrounding covert operations, shedding light on the moral dilemmas faced by governments and the potential impact on international relations.

Repercussions for U.S. foreign policy and international relations

The subchapter titled "Repercussions for U.S. foreign policy and international relations" delves into the far-reaching consequences of Operation Northwoods and its implications for the United States' role on the global stage. This section explores how the controversial project, which aimed to orchestrate a pretext for military intervention in Cuba, has shaped the course of U.S. foreign policy and international relations.

One of the key areas of focus in this subchapter is the political ramifications and controversies surrounding Operation Northwoods. Historians examine how the revelation of this covert operation has affected public trust in government institutions and raised questions about the ethical boundaries of U.S. military strategies. The subchapter also delves into the decision-making process behind Operation Northwoods, providing a historical analysis of the factors that led to its proposal and subsequent abandonment.

Furthermore, this section highlights the role of the military-industrial complex in planning Operation Northwoods. By exploring the connections between defense contractors, the military, and policymakers, historians shed light on the influence wielded by these actors in shaping U.S. military strategies. Comparisons with other covert operations in U.S. history are drawn to provide a broader context and understand how Operation Northwoods fits into the larger framework of American foreign policy.

The impact of Operation Northwoods on U.S.-Cuba relations is another focal point of this subchapter. Historians explore how this failed military intervention project affected diplomatic ties between the two nations, including the potential for escalation and the subsequent pursuit of alternative strategies. The legacy of Operation Northwoods in shaping future military strategies is also examined, with a particular emphasis on the lessons learned and the subsequent evolution of psychological warfare and propaganda tactics.

Intelligence agencies play a significant role in planning and executing covert operations like Operation Northwoods, and this subchapter delves into their involvement. The subchapter explores the inner workings of intelligence agencies, their motivations, and the methodologies employed in executing such operations.

Lastly, the international response to the declassification of Operation Northwoods documents is explored. This section analyzes how the revelation of this covert operation has impacted the United States' standing in the international community, including its credibility as a global leader and its ability to foster cooperation and trust with other nations.

In conclusion, the subchapter "Repercussions for U.S. foreign policy and international relations" offers a comprehensive analysis of the wide-ranging consequences of Operation Northwoods. By addressing the various aspects of this failed covert operation, historians gain valuable insights into the historical impact of this event and its enduring significance in shaping U.S. foreign policy and international relations.

Chapter 4: Historical analysis of the decision-making process behind Operation Northwoods

Examination of the events and factors that led to the conception of Operation Northwoods

In this subchapter, we delve into the fascinating and controversial history surrounding the conception of Operation Northwoods. Historians and those interested in the intricacies of this infamous covert operation will find this examination enlightening and thought-provoking.

To truly understand the origins of Operation Northwoods, we must first explore the historical context and factors that contributed to its inception. The early 1960s were a tumultuous time in U.S.-Cuba relations, with tensions escalating between the two nations. The Bay of Pigs invasion in 1961 had failed, leaving a bitter taste in the mouths of U.S. policymakers who were eager to find alternative means to combat the perceived threat of communism in Cuba.

Conspiracy theories surrounding Operation Northwoods have circulated for decades, leading to widespread speculation and intrigue. This subchapter carefully dissects these theories, separating fact from fiction and shedding light on the motivations and intentions behind the operation.

The political ramifications and controversies of Operation Northwoods cannot be ignored. The revelation of this covert operation, which involved proposing false flag attacks on U.S. soil to justify military intervention in Cuba, shocked the public and led to questions about the ethics and morality of such actions. We explore the aftermath of the operation, including the political fallout and the impact it had on U.S.-Cuba relations.

To gain a comprehensive understanding of Operation Northwoods, a historical analysis of the decision-making process is crucial. This subchapter examines the key players involved in the planning and execution of the operation, as well as the factors that influenced their decision-making. We explore the role of the military-industrial complex in shaping the operation and its implications for future military strategies.

Comparisons between Operation Northwoods and other covert operations in U.S. history provide valuable insights into the broader patterns of government behavior. By examining the similarities and differences, we can better understand the motivations behind such operations and the potential long-term consequences.

The impact of Operation Northwoods on U.S.-Cuba relations cannot be overstated. This subchapter explores the immediate and long-term effects of the operation on diplomatic relations between the two nations, as well as the legacy it left behind in shaping future military strategies.

Psychological warfare and propaganda tactics proposed in Operation Northwoods are analyzed, shedding light on the strategies employed by intelligence agencies during this period. This examination provides valuable insights into the inner workings of covert operations and their implications for modern-day intelligence practices.

The role of intelligence agencies in planning and executing covert operations like Operation Northwoods is a topic of great interest to historians and those studying the complexities of government actions. This subchapter explores the involvement of various intelligence agencies in the planning and execution of Operation Northwoods, providing a detailed analysis of their roles and responsibilities.

Finally, we examine the international response to the declassification of Operation Northwoods documents. This subchapter analyzes the global reactions to the revelation of this covert operation, exploring the implications it had on international relations and the broader perception of U.S. foreign policy.

By thoroughly examining the events and factors that led to the conception of Operation Northwoods, this subchapter aims to provide historians and those interested in this historical period with a comprehensive and nuanced understanding of this infamous covert operation.

Evaluation of the decision-making process within the U.S. government

The decision-making process within the U.S. government has always been a topic of interest for historians, especially when it comes to covert operations and controversial events. One such event that continues to intrigue researchers is Operation Northwoods, the 1962 U.S. project for military intervention in Cuba that was never implemented. This subchapter aims to provide a comprehensive evaluation of the decision-making process behind Operation Northwoods, shedding light on its political ramifications, historical analysis, and the role of various stakeholders.

In order to understand the decision-making process behind Operation Northwoods, it is essential to delve into the conspiracy theories surrounding it. Historians have long debated the motives and intentions of the U.S. government in planning such an operation, and this subchapter will explore the various theories put forth by experts in the field.

Furthermore, the political ramifications and controversies of Operation Northwoods cannot be overlooked. The potential impact on U.S.-Cuba relations and the international community's response to the declassification of Operation Northwoods documents are crucial aspects that will be examined in this subchapter.

A historical analysis of the decision-making process will provide valuable insights into the factors that influenced the planning and execution of Operation Northwoods. By comparing it to other covert operations in U.S. history, historians can gain a deeper understanding of the context and significance of this operation.

The role of the military-industrial complex in planning Operation Northwoods is another important aspect that will be explored. This subchapter aims to shed light on the influence of defense contractors and the implications of their involvement in shaping military strategies.

Moreover, Operation Northwoods' impact on future military strategies cannot be underestimated. By examining its legacy, historians can assess how this operation shaped subsequent covert operations and psychological warfare and propaganda tactics.

The subchapter will also address the role of intelligence agencies in planning and executing covert operations like Operation Northwoods. By analyzing their involvement, historians can gain insights into the decision-making dynamics within these agencies and their interactions with the broader government apparatus.

Finally, the international response to the declassification of Operation Northwoods documents will be examined. This subchapter will shed light on how this revelation impacted U.S.-Cuba relations and the broader international community's perception of the U.S. government's covert activities.

In conclusion, this subchapter provides a comprehensive evaluation of the decision-making process within the U.S. government, focusing on Operation Northwoods. By exploring its historical context, political ramifications, and the role of various stakeholders, historians can gain valuable insights into this controversial event and its broader implications.

Analysis of the internal discussions and debates surrounding Operation Northwoods

In this subchapter, we delve into the intricate internal discussions and debates that took place within the United States government surrounding Operation Northwoods. This covert project, devised in 1962, aimed to justify military intervention in Cuba, but was ultimately never implemented. Historians have long been intrigued by the behind-the-scenes conversations and political maneuvering that occurred during this critical period.

One of the key aspects we explore is the conspiracy theories that have emerged surrounding Operation Northwoods. These theories suggest that the project was not simply an isolated incident, but rather part of a larger pattern of covert operations and manipulation by the U.S. government. We examine the evidence supporting and debunking these theories, shedding light on the motivations behind Operation Northwoods.

Furthermore, we analyze the political ramifications and controversies that surrounded this operation. The decision-making process behind Operation Northwoods is scrutinized, with a focus on the individuals involved and the influence of political agendas. This analysis provides valuable insights into the inner workings of the U.S. government during this period.

A historical perspective is crucial in understanding Operation Northwoods. By examining past covert operations, we draw comparisons and highlight similarities and differences between Operation Northwoods and other significant events in U.S. history. This contextualization allows us to better comprehend the significance of

Operation Northwoods in shaping future military strategies and policies.

We also explore the role of the military-industrial complex in planning Operation Northwoods, shedding light on the influence of defense contractors and the defense industry on government decision-making. This analysis provides a deeper understanding of the complex relationship between the military and the private sector.

The psychological warfare and propaganda tactics proposed in Operation Northwoods are examined in detail. By analyzing the strategies devised to manipulate public opinion and justify military intervention, we gain insights into the mindset and tactics employed by intelligence agencies during this period.

Lastly, we delve into the international response to the declassification of Operation Northwoods documents. The impact of this revelation on U.S.-Cuba relations is assessed, as well as the wider implications for international relations and transparency in government.

This subchapter provides historians and those interested in Operation Northwoods with a comprehensive analysis of the internal discussions and debates that surrounded this controversial project. By exploring the political, historical, and international dimensions of Operation Northwoods, we shed light on its significance and legacy in shaping U.S. military strategies and policies.

Impact of historical context and prevailing ideologies on the decision-making process

The Impact of Historical Context and Prevailing Ideologies on the Decision-Making Process

In the subchapter titled "Impact of historical context and prevailing ideologies on the decision-making process," we delve into the intricate relationship between historical events, prevailing ideologies, and the decision-making process behind Operation Northwoods. This chapter aims to provide a comprehensive understanding of how external factors shaped the controversial U.S. project for military intervention in Cuba in 1962.

To grasp the full scope of Operation Northwoods, it is crucial to explore the historical context in which it emerged. By analyzing the political, social, and economic climate of the time, historians can gain insights into the factors that influenced decision-makers. Understanding the Cold War dynamics, the heightened tensions between the United States and Cuba, and the broader geopolitical landscape is essential for a comprehensive analysis.

Furthermore, prevailing ideologies played a significant role in shaping the decision-making process. This subchapter highlights the various political ramifications and controversies surrounding Operation Northwoods. It explores how different ideological perspectives, such as anti-communism and the military-industrial complex, influenced the project's planning and execution. By examining the role of intelligence agencies and the psychological warfare and propaganda tactics proposed, historians can assess the extent to which prevailing ideologies impacted the decision-making process.

Comparative analysis between Operation Northwoods and other covert operations in U.S. history also provides valuable insights. By examining similarities and differences, historians can identify patterns in decision-making, evaluate the effectiveness of covert operations, and explore the long-term consequences of such endeavors.

Moreover, this subchapter explores the impact of Operation Northwoods on U.S.-Cuba relations. By examining the international response to the declassification of Operation Northwoods documents, historians can evaluate how the project affected diplomatic relations and shaped future military strategies.

Finally, this chapter examines the legacy of Operation Northwoods in shaping future military strategies. By analyzing the project's outcomes and the subsequent changes in decision-making processes, historians can trace the long-term effects and lessons learned from this controversial endeavor.

Overall, this subchapter provides a detailed exploration of the impact of historical context and prevailing ideologies on the decision-making process behind Operation Northwoods. By delving into the historical analysis, political ramifications, and controversies surrounding the project, historians gain a comprehensive understanding of this pivotal moment in U.S.-Cuba relations and its broader implications on military strategies.

Chapter 5: The role of the military-industrial complex in planning Operation Northwoods

Introduction to the military-industrial complex and its influence on U.S. military strategies

The military-industrial complex has played a significant role in shaping U.S. military strategies throughout history. This subchapter aims to provide historians with an in-depth understanding of the complex and its influence on one particular event - Operation Northwoods, a controversial U.S. project for military intervention in Cuba that was never implemented.

Operation Northwoods, which took place in 1962, was a covert operation proposed by the U.S. Department of Defense and the Joint Chiefs of Staff. It aimed to create a pretext for a military intervention in Cuba, targeting Fidel Castro's regime. The operation involved various sinister tactics, including false flag attacks, staged acts of terrorism, and even the possibility of sacrificing American lives to justify military action.

Conspiracy theories surrounding Operation Northwoods have captivated the imagination of many, raising questions about the extent of the government's involvement in planning such operations. This subchapter will delve into the political ramifications and controversies surrounding Operation Northwoods, exploring the decision-making process behind this audacious plan.

One cannot analyze Operation Northwoods without considering the role of the military-industrial complex. This influential network of defense contractors, government agencies, and policymakers has long been accused of shaping military strategies to serve their own economic interests. By examining the involvement of the military-industrial complex in planning Operation Northwoods, historians can gain valuable insights into the interplay between political motivations, corporate interests, and military actions.

Furthermore, this subchapter will draw comparisons between Operation Northwoods and other covert operations in U.S. history, shedding light on the patterns and strategies employed by the military-industrial complex in orchestrating such operations.

The impact of Operation Northwoods on U.S.-Cuba relations cannot be overstated. Although the operation was never executed, it had profound implications for the relationship between the two nations. Historians will explore the repercussions of this failed operation and its lasting effects on subsequent military strategies.

Additionally, the subchapter will delve into the psychological warfare and propaganda tactics proposed in Operation Northwoods, highlighting the lengths to which the military-industrial complex was willing to go to achieve its objectives.

Furthermore, the role of intelligence agencies in planning and executing covert operations like Operation Northwoods will be examined, shedding light on the intricate web of secrecy and power that surrounds such endeavors.

Finally, historians will delve into the international response to the declassification of Operation Northwoods documents, exploring how this revelation shaped global perceptions of U.S. military strategies and the military-industrial complex.

By thoroughly examining the military-industrial complex's influence on Operation Northwoods and its wider implications, historians can gain a deeper understanding of the complex dynamics that have shaped U.S. military strategies throughout history.

Examination of the defense industry's involvement in planning Operation Northwoods

Operation Northwoods was a top-secret project developed in 1962 by the United States government, aimed at justifying military intervention in Cuba. Although the operation was never implemented, it has become a subject of intrigue and controversy, leading historians to delve into its various aspects. One crucial aspect that warrants examination is the defense industry's involvement in planning Operation Northwoods.

The defense industry, comprising private companies involved in the production of military equipment and services, has long been intertwined with the government's military strategies. In the case of Operation Northwoods, it is important to understand the extent to which defense contractors played a role in shaping the operation's objectives and tactics.

Historians have scrutinized declassified documents and unearthed evidence suggesting that defense industry representatives actively participated in the planning of Operation Northwoods. These documents reveal a disturbing level of collaboration between defense contractors and government officials, raising questions about the influence of the military-industrial complex on national security decisions.

The military-industrial complex, a term popularized by President Dwight D. Eisenhower, refers to the close relationship between the military establishment, the defense industry, and the government. Operation Northwoods serves as a historical case study highlighting the complex dynamics within this relationship.

Comparisons between Operation Northwoods and other covert operations in U.S. history reveal patterns of collusion between the defense industry and the government. The defense industry's involvement suggests that profit motives and political agendas may have influenced the decision-making process behind Operation Northwoods.

The legacy of Operation Northwoods extends beyond its immediate historical context. The operation's proposed psychological warfare and propaganda tactics shed light on the strategies employed by intelligence agencies in planning covert operations. Understanding the role of intelligence agencies in executing operations like Northwoods is crucial for comprehending the broader implications of such endeavors.

Furthermore, the international response to the declassification of Operation Northwoods documents provides valuable insights into the global perception of the United States' covert activities. The revelation of a proposed false flag operation aimed at justifying military aggression in Cuba undoubtedly influenced U.S.-Cuba relations and sparked international discussions about the ethics of covert operations.

In conclusion, the examination of the defense industry's involvement in planning Operation Northwoods is a vital component of understanding this controversial project. By analyzing the historical impact of the military-industrial complex, scrutinizing the decision-making process, and exploring the implications for future military strategies, historians can shed light on the intricate dynamics between the defense industry, government, and intelligence agencies. Ultimately, this examination contributes to a comprehensive understanding of Operation Northwoods and its significance in U.S.-Cuba relations.

Analysis of the potential motivations and interests of the military-industrial complex

The military-industrial complex has long been a subject of interest and speculation among historians, particularly when it comes to covert operations like Operation Northwoods. This subchapter aims to delve into the potential motivations and interests that may have driven the military-industrial complex to plan such an audacious operation.

One of the primary motivations behind the military-industrial complex's involvement in Operation Northwoods can be traced back to economic interests. The military-industrial complex is a powerful network of defense contractors, government officials, and the armed forces, which relies heavily on military spending for its profitability. By creating a climate of fear and aggression towards Cuba, the military-industrial complex could have expected a surge in defense spending, leading to substantial financial gains for its constituents.

Furthermore, the military-industrial complex's desire to maintain its influence and control over U.S. foreign policy cannot be overlooked. Operation Northwoods was conceived during a period of intense Cold War tensions, where the U.S. was engaged in a global struggle for supremacy with the Soviet Union. By planning a covert operation against Cuba, the military-industrial complex sought to assert its dominance in shaping U.S. foreign policy and demonstrate its indispensability in the face of perceived threats.

Additionally, the military-industrial complex's involvement in Operation Northwoods can be seen as a manifestation of its eagerness to test and showcase its military capabilities. This complex thrives on innovation and the development of advanced weaponry. Operation Northwoods presented an opportunity to experiment with new technologies and tactics, thereby solidifying the position of defense contractors and military leaders who wanted to showcase their capabilities to potential buyers and allies.

Moreover, the military-industrial complex's close ties with intelligence agencies played a significant role in shaping Operation Northwoods. The collaboration between defense contractors, military officials, and intelligence agencies allowed for the exchange of information, resources, and expertise necessary for planning and executing covert operations. The military-industrial complex's interests aligned with those of intelligence agencies, as both sought to expand their influence and maintain the perception of a constant threat, justifying their existence and funding.

In conclusion, the motivations and interests of the military-industrial complex in planning Operation Northwoods were multifaceted. Economic interests, desire for control over U.S. foreign policy, the need to showcase military capabilities, and collaboration with intelligence agencies all played a role in shaping the complex's involvement. By understanding these motivations, historians can gain valuable insights into the inner workings of the military-industrial complex and its impact on U.S.-Cuba relations and covert operations throughout history.

Implications for democratic governance and civilian control over military actions

In the subchapter "Implications for democratic governance and civilian control over military actions" of the book "Operation Northwoods and U.S.-Cuba Relations: A Historical Impact," we delve into the profound consequences that this controversial project had on the democratic governance of the United States and the preservation of civilian control over military actions.

Operation Northwoods, a classified project proposed in 1962, aimed to create a pretext for military intervention in Cuba. Although never implemented, the implications of this project cannot be underestimated. One of the key aspects explored in this subchapter is the alarming erosion of democratic principles and the potential threat to civilian control over military actions.

The decision-making process behind Operation Northwoods raises questions about the extent of transparency, accountability, and checks and balances within the U.S. government. By analyzing the historical context, we gain insights into the political ramifications and controversies surrounding this covert operation. This subchapter meticulously examines the role of various government entities, intelligence agencies, and the military-industrial complex in planning and executing Operation Northwoods.

Furthermore, the comparison between Operation Northwoods and other covert operations in U.S. history helps historians understand the significance of this project in shaping future military strategies. By studying the psychological warfare and propaganda tactics proposed in Operation Northwoods, we gain a deeper understanding of the potential manipulation of public opinion and the ethical implications of such strategies.

The impact of Operation Northwoods on U.S.-Cuba relations cannot be overlooked. The declassification of Operation Northwoods documents triggered an international response, highlighting the delicate nature of covert operations and their potential to strain diplomatic ties. Historians will find an in-depth analysis of the international response to these declassified documents, shedding light on the global perception and repercussions of such secretive military projects.

Ultimately, this subchapter serves as a vital resource for historians, offering a comprehensive exploration of the implications of Operation Northwoods on democratic governance, civilian control over military actions, and the broader political landscape. By examining the historical impact and legacy of this covert operation, we gain valuable insights into the delicate balance between national security interests, democratic principles, and the responsible exercise of military power.

Chapter 6: Comparisons between Operation Northwoods and other covert operations in U.S. history

Overview of significant covert operations in U.S. history

Covert operations have played a significant role in shaping the course of U.S. history. These secret missions, often conducted by intelligence agencies or military organizations, have had far-reaching consequences and have sometimes been shrouded in controversy. One such operation that stands out in American history is Operation Northwoods, a project that was never implemented but had a profound impact on U.S.-Cuba relations and military strategy.

Operation Northwoods was a covert plan devised by the U.S. Department of Defense in 1962. It aimed to justify a military intervention in Cuba by staging false-flag attacks on American soil and blaming them on the Cuban government. The project proposed various psychological warfare and propaganda tactics, including hijacking planes, sinking ships, and even orchestrating terrorist attacks against U.S. citizens. The intention was to create a pretext for a military invasion of Cuba and the removal of Fidel Castro's regime.

The revelation of Operation Northwoods documents has fueled conspiracy theories surrounding the motives and intentions of the U.S. government. Critics argue that the project demonstrates the willingness of the U.S. to engage in deceit and manipulation to further its political agenda. The decision-making process behind Operation Northwoods has been subject to historical analysis, shedding light on the complex dynamics between intelligence agencies, military leaders, and political figures.

Comparisons have been drawn between Operation Northwoods and other covert operations in U.S. history, such as the infamous Bay of Pigs invasion and the Gulf of Tonkin incident. These cases highlight the recurring theme of secrecy, hidden agendas, and the role of the military-industrial complex in shaping U.S. foreign policy.

The impact of Operation Northwoods on U.S.-Cuba relations cannot be underestimated. While the operation was never implemented, it left a lasting legacy in shaping future military strategies and tactics. It also strained U.S.-Cuba relations, heightening tensions and reinforcing the already deep-rooted hostilities between the two nations.

The declassification of Operation Northwoods documents sparked an international response, with many countries expressing concern over the U.S. government's willingness to engage in covert operations. The role of intelligence agencies in planning and executing such missions has come under scrutiny, raising questions about transparency and accountability.

As historians delve into the intricacies of covert operations like Operation Northwoods, it becomes increasingly clear that these clandestine activities have had a profound impact on the course of U.S. history. Understanding the political ramifications, controversies, and decision-making processes behind these operations is crucial to comprehending the complex dynamics that have shaped American foreign policy.

Comparative analysis of Operation Northwoods with previous covert operations

The subchapter titled "Comparative analysis of Operation Northwoods with previous covert operations" delves into the historical context and sheds light on the similarities and differences between Operation Northwoods and previous covert operations conducted by the United States government. This analysis aims to provide historians with a comprehensive understanding of the decision-making processes, political ramifications, and long-term impacts of such operations.

One notable aspect to consider is the role of the military-industrial complex in planning Operation Northwoods and its connection to previous covert operations. By examining past instances such as the Bay of Pigs invasion and the Iran-Contra affair, a clearer picture emerges of how influential military interests can shape covert operations and their objectives. Understanding these connections can shed light on the motivations behind Operation Northwoods and the potential influences that external actors may have had on its planning and execution.

Another crucial aspect to explore is the psychological warfare and propaganda tactics proposed in Operation Northwoods, comparing them to similar strategies employed in previous covert operations. This analysis will provide historians with insights into the evolution of psychological warfare techniques and their utilization in shaping public opinion, both domestically and internationally. By examining the historical context, historians can evaluate the effectiveness of these tactics and their impact on public perception and political decision-making.

Furthermore, it is essential to examine the international response to the declassification of Operation Northwoods documents and compare it to the reactions following the exposure of other covert operations. This analysis will highlight the differing reactions from various stakeholders, including foreign governments, international organizations, and the general public. Understanding these responses can provide historians with valuable insights into the global perception of covert operations and their implications for international relations.

By conducting a comparative analysis of Operation Northwoods with previous covert operations, historians can gain a deeper understanding of the historical impact of such operations. This analysis will contribute to the broader understanding of U.S.-Cuba relations, the decision-making processes behind covert operations, the role of intelligence agencies, and the legacy of Operation Northwoods in shaping future military strategies. Ultimately, this subchapter aims to provide historians with a comprehensive and nuanced perspective on Operation Northwoods and its place within the broader historical context of covert operations.

Examination of similarities and differences in objectives, strategies, and outcomes

In this subchapter, we delve into a comprehensive examination of the similarities and differences in objectives, strategies, and outcomes between Operation Northwoods and other covert operations in U.S. history. This analysis aims to provide historians with a deeper understanding of the historical impact of Operation Northwoods and its significance in U.S.-Cuba relations.

Firstly, we explore the objectives behind Operation Northwoods, the 1962 U.S. project for military intervention in Cuba that was never implemented. By examining declassified documents and testimonies, we shed light on the intended goals of this operation, such as generating public support for a military intervention and justifying the overthrow of Fidel Castro's regime. Comparisons are drawn between these objectives and those of other covert operations, highlighting common themes and unique motivations.

Next, we delve into the strategies employed in Operation Northwoods and how they differ from other covert operations. This section focuses on the proposed psychological warfare and propaganda tactics, which aimed to manipulate public opinion and create a pretext for military intervention. By analyzing the specific strategies proposed in Operation Northwoods as well as those employed in other covert operations throughout history, historians gain insights into the evolving nature of psychological warfare and propaganda tactics.

The outcomes of Operation Northwoods and its impact on U.S.-Cuba relations are also critically examined. By exploring the political ramifications and controversies surrounding this operation, historians can assess its long-term effects on bilateral relations and the broader geopolitical landscape. Additionally, we analyze the international response to the declassification of Operation Northwoods documents, shedding light on how this revelation impacted global perceptions of U.S. covert operations.

Furthermore, we explore the historical analysis of the decision-making process behind Operation Northwoods, taking into account the role of the military-industrial complex in planning this operation. By examining the intricate web of actors, interests, and motivations involved, historians gain a deeper understanding of the complex dynamics that shaped covert operations during this period.

Finally, we discuss the legacy of Operation Northwoods in shaping future military strategies. By drawing comparisons between this operation and subsequent covert operations, historians can identify patterns and trends in U.S. military planning. This analysis sheds light on how Operation Northwoods influenced subsequent strategies and its lasting impact on the evolution of U.S. military doctrine.

Overall, this subchapter provides historians with a comprehensive examination of the similarities and differences in objectives, strategies, and outcomes between Operation Northwoods and other covert operations in U.S. history. By addressing the various niches surrounding Operation Northwoods, historians can gain valuable insights into the historical impact of this operation and its significance in shaping U.S.-Cuba relations and broader military strategies.

Lessons learned from past covert operations and their application to future decision-making

Covert operations have long played a significant role in shaping the course of history, often with far-reaching consequences. Understanding the lessons learned from these operations can provide invaluable insights into future decision-making processes. In the context of Operation Northwoods and its impact on U.S.-Cuba relations, historians can delve into a range of fascinating topics that shed light on the intricacies of covert operations and their implications.

One of the most intriguing aspects of Operation Northwoods is the conspiracy theories that surround it. By examining these theories, historians can analyze the complex web of political ramifications and controversies that have arisen from covert operations throughout history. This analysis can help identify patterns and recurring themes, providing valuable lessons on the potential pitfalls of such operations.

Furthermore, a historical analysis of the decision-making process behind Operation Northwoods can offer valuable insights into the dynamics between the military, intelligence agencies, and political leaders. This exploration can shed light on the influence of the military-industrial complex in planning covert operations and the ethical considerations involved.

Comparisons between Operation Northwoods and other covert operations in U.S. history can also provide historians with a broader understanding of the strategic thinking and tactics employed throughout the years. By examining the various approaches taken in different operations, historians can identify successful strategies and techniques that can be applied to future decision-making processes.

Operation Northwoods also offers a unique opportunity to explore the psychological warfare and propaganda tactics proposed in its planning.

Understanding these tactics and their potential impact can inform future strategies in the realm of information warfare, particularly in the age of social media and digital communication.

The declassification of Operation Northwoods documents has sparked international interest and prompted a response from various countries. Investigating the international response to these documents can offer insights into the global perceptions of covert operations and their impact on diplomatic relations.

Ultimately, the legacy of Operation Northwoods in shaping future military strategies cannot be underestimated. By studying this operation, historians can draw valuable lessons on the ethical considerations, decision-making processes, and long-term consequences of covert operations. These lessons can inform future policies and strategies, ensuring that history is not repeated and that decision-makers are better equipped to navigate the complexities of covert operations in the future.

Chapter 7: The impact of Operation Northwoods on U.S.-Cuba relations

Immediate effects on U.S.-Cuba relations following the revelation of Operation Northwoods

The revelation of Operation Northwoods in the early 2000s had significant immediate effects on U.S.-Cuba relations. Operation Northwoods, a classified 1962 U.S. project for military intervention in Cuba that was never implemented, was met with shock and disbelief when its documents were declassified.

For historians, the unveiling of Operation Northwoods shed light on the depths of the Cold War era and the extreme measures considered by the U.S. government. The conspiracy theories surrounding Operation Northwoods were finally put to rest as undeniable evidence of the project's existence came to light.

The political ramifications and controversies of Operation Northwoods were immense. The revelation sparked outrage among many, both domestically and internationally. Critics argued that the project exemplified the dangerous lengths the U.S. was willing to go to achieve its political objectives, even at the expense of innocent lives. This revelation fueled existing skepticism about U.S. foreign policy and its intentions towards Cuba.

The historical analysis of the decision-making process behind Operation Northwoods became a subject of intense scrutiny. Historians delved into the motives and rationale of the military and intelligence officials involved in planning the operation. The role of the military-industrial complex in shaping the project also came under examination, as many questioned the influence of defense contractors and their vested interests in perpetuating conflicts.

Comparisons between Operation Northwoods and other covert operations in U.S. history were drawn. Historians sought to understand if this project was an aberration or part of a larger pattern of deception and manipulation in U.S. foreign policy. The impact of Operation Northwoods on U.S.-Cuba relations was undeniable, as it deepened the mistrust between the two nations and further strained diplomatic efforts.

Operation Northwoods also left a lasting legacy in shaping future military strategies. The project's proposals for psychological warfare and propaganda tactics were alarming to many, highlighting the potential dangers of manipulating public opinion. This revelation underscored the need for greater oversight and accountability in intelligence agencies' planning and execution of covert operations.

Internationally, the declassification of Operation Northwoods documents sparked condemnation and concern. The international response focused on the implications for global peace and stability, as well as the erosion of trust in the U.S. government. It served as a reminder of the importance of transparency and international cooperation in preventing similar incidents in the future.

In conclusion, the immediate effects on U.S.-Cuba relations following the revelation of Operation Northwoods were profound. It exposed the dark underbelly of U.S. foreign policy and raised crucial questions about the balance between national security and ethical considerations. The legacy of Operation Northwoods continues to shape historical analysis, military strategies, and international perceptions of U.S. actions.

Long-term consequences for diplomatic relations and bilateral cooperation

The subchapter titled "Long-term consequences for diplomatic relations and bilateral cooperation" delves into the enduring impact of Operation

Northwoods on the relationship between the United States and Cuba. This section explores how the controversial project, which aimed to justify a military intervention in Cuba through false flag operations, continues to shape diplomatic dynamics between the two countries. Historians and those interested in the intricacies of Operation Northwoods will find this analysis crucial in understanding the far-reaching consequences of the project.

The chapter commences by examining the immediate aftermath of the declassification of Operation Northwoods documents. The international response to these revelations, including from Cuba and other nations, is thoroughly explored. By shedding light on the global reaction, historians gain insight into the perception of the United States' covert operations and the potential damage to diplomatic trust.

Furthermore, this section delves into the long-term implications of the project on bilateral cooperation between the United States and Cuba. It elucidates how Operation Northwoods has perpetuated mistrust and suspicion, hindering any prospects of meaningful collaboration. The project's exposure has left a lasting scar on the diplomatic relationship, making it imperative for historians to study its repercussions on future negotiations and cooperation.

In addition, this subchapter delves into the broader historical context of covert operations and their impact on diplomatic relations. By comparing Operation Northwoods to other clandestine missions in U.S. history, historians can discern patterns and trends in the conduct of such operations. This comparative analysis offers valuable insights into the decision-making process behind Operation Northwoods and its broader implications for foreign policy.

The subchapter concludes by addressing the role of intelligence agencies in planning and executing covert operations such as Operation Northwoods. By examining the involvement of these agencies, historians can evaluate the extent to which these operations influence diplomatic relations. This analysis sheds light on the intricate web of intelligence, propaganda, and psychological warfare tactics employed to shape public opinion and secure political objectives.

Overall, this subchapter provides a comprehensive analysis of the long-term consequences of Operation Northwoods. By exploring the project's impact on diplomatic relations, bilateral cooperation, and the broader historical landscape, historians gain a deep understanding of its historical significance and ongoing ramifications.

Examination of the Cuban perspective and response to Operation Northwoods

The subchapter titled "Examination of the Cuban perspective and response to Operation Northwoods" delves into the Cuban government's reaction to the revelation of Operation Northwoods. This section provides a comprehensive analysis of how the Cuban perspective shaped their response and influenced U.S.-Cuba relations.

From a historical standpoint, it is crucial to understand Operation Northwoods as a pivotal event in U.S.-Cuba relations. The Cuban government's perspective on this covert operation was deeply rooted in the historical context of their strained relationship with the United States. Understanding this perspective provides valuable insight into their response.

One key aspect to consider is the conspiracy theories surrounding Operation Northwoods. The Cuban government, suspicious of U.S. intentions, viewed these theories as further evidence of a long-standing hostile agenda. This suspicion influenced their response and their decision-making process.

The political ramifications and controversies of Operation Northwoods also played a significant role in shaping the Cuban perspective. The covert nature of the operation, which involved plans for false flag attacks, psychological warfare, and propaganda tactics, raised concerns about the U.S. government's intentions and credibility.

Furthermore, the role of the military-industrial complex in planning Operation Northwoods cannot be understated. The Cuban government perceived this as evidence of a powerful and influential group pushing for military intervention in Cuba. This realization undoubtedly shaped their response and subsequent actions.

Comparisons between Operation Northwoods and other covert operations in U.S. history provide further context for the Cuban perspective. By examining similar operations, historians can gain a better understanding of the Cuban government's response and the impact of Operation Northwoods on U.S.-Cuba relations.

The declassification of Operation Northwoods documents had a significant impact on the international community. This subchapter analyzes the international response to these revelations and how it affected global perceptions of the United States and its foreign policies.

In conclusion, the examination of the Cuban perspective and response to Operation Northwoods offers historians a deeper understanding of the complex dynamics between the United States and Cuba. By exploring the historical impact of this covert operation, historians can assess its role in shaping future military strategies and its enduring legacy in U.S.-Cuba relations. The subchapter sheds light on the psychological warfare and propaganda tactics proposed in Operation Northwoods, the role of intelligence agencies in planning and executing such covert operations, and the broader implications for international relations.

Implications for regional stability and the broader Cold

War context

The subchapter titled "Implications for regional stability and the broader Cold War context" delves into the far-reaching consequences of Operation Northwoods, exploring how this covert U.S. military intervention project impacted both regional stability and the broader geopolitical landscape during the Cold War era.

Within the context of regional stability, Operation Northwoods threatened to disrupt the delicate balance of power in the Americas. By planning a series of false flag attacks on Cuban targets and attributing them to the Cuban government, the U.S. aimed to create a pretext for military intervention in Cuba. This not only risked destabilizing the Cuban regime but also had the potential to ignite a broader conflict in the region, drawing in other nations and potentially escalating the already tense Cold War dynamics.

Furthermore, the implications of Operation Northwoods extended beyond the immediate regional context, as it shed light on the broader strategies employed by the U.S. during the Cold War. By examining the decision-making process behind Operation Northwoods, historians can gain valuable insights into the mindset and motivations of U.S. policymakers during this period. This historical analysis allows for a deeper understanding of the political ramifications and controversies surrounding covert operations like Operation Northwoods, shedding light on the complex interplay between national security, ideology, and foreign policy objectives.

Comparisons between Operation Northwoods and other covert operations in U.S. history also contribute to a comprehensive understanding of the broader Cold War context. By examining similarities and differences between Operation Northwoods and other operations, such as the Bay of Pigs invasion or the Iran-Contra affair, historians can identify patterns in U.S. military strategies and evaluate the long-term impact of these operations on U.S. foreign policy.

Moreover, the legacy of Operation Northwoods in shaping future military strategies cannot be underestimated. The declassification of Operation Northwoods documents triggered international responses and raised questions about the role of intelligence agencies in planning and executing covert operations. Historians can analyze the international response to these revelations, examining how they shaped public perceptions, diplomatic relations, and the broader discourse surrounding U.S.-Cuba relations.

In conclusion, the subchapter "Implications for regional stability and the broader Cold War context" explores the profound impact of Operation Northwoods on both regional stability and the broader Cold War dynamics. By examining the historical, political, and strategic dimensions of this covert operation, historians gain valuable insights into the decision-making processes, the role of intelligence agencies, and the long-term consequences of such operations. Ultimately, this subchapter contributes to a deeper understanding of the historical impact of Operation Northwoods and its significance within the broader narrative of U.S.-Cuba relations and the Cold War era.

Chapter 8: The legacy of Operation Northwoods in shaping future military strategies

Evaluation of the impact of Operation Northwoods on subsequent U.S. military planning

Operation Northwoods, a secret military project proposed in 1962, aimed to create a pretext for a U.S. military intervention in Cuba. Although the operation was never carried out, its historical impact on subsequent U.S. military planning cannot be underestimated. This subchapter delves into the evaluation of that impact, analyzing how Operation Northwoods influenced future military strategies and planning.

One of the significant aspects to consider is the conspiracy theories surrounding Operation Northwoods. Historians have extensively explored these theories, which suggest that the operation's proposal reveals a dark side of U.S. government and military intentions. By examining these conspiracy theories, historians can shed light on the political ramifications and controversies of Operation Northwoods, allowing for a more comprehensive understanding of its impact.

Furthermore, a historical analysis of the decision-making process behind Operation Northwoods is crucial in evaluating its impact. By examining the motivations and justifications put forth by military officials during that time, historians can assess how the project influenced subsequent military planning. This analysis allows for a deeper understanding of the role of the military-industrial complex in planning Operation Northwoods and its effect on future military strategies.

Comparisons between Operation Northwoods and other covert operations in U.S. history also provide valuable insights. By examining similarities and differences, historians can evaluate how the project shaped subsequent military strategies and tactics. This comparative analysis enables a comprehensive understanding of the legacy of Operation Northwoods in shaping future military planning.

Additionally, the subchapter explores the psychological warfare and propaganda tactics proposed in Operation Northwoods. By examining these tactics, historians can assess their potential influence on subsequent military planning and operations. This evaluation contributes to understanding the role of intelligence agencies in planning and executing covert operations like Operation Northwoods.

Finally, the subchapter addresses the international response to the declassification of Operation Northwoods documents. By analyzing the reactions of other countries to the project's revelations, historians can evaluate the global impact and implications of Operation Northwoods.

Overall, the evaluation of the impact of Operation Northwoods on subsequent U.S. military planning provides historians with valuable insights into the political, strategic, and historical consequences of this secret military project. By examining the project's influence on decision-making processes, military tactics, and international relations, historians can gain a comprehensive understanding of its historical significance.

Analysis of the influence of Operation Northwoods on the development of unconventional warfare tactics

Operation Northwoods was a highly controversial and secretive project developed by the United States in 1962, with the intention of justifying military intervention in Cuba. Although never implemented, this project had a profound impact on the development of unconventional warfare tactics and continues to be a subject of interest for historians.

One of the key aspects to analyze is the influence of Operation Northwoods on the subsequent use of conspiracy theories in covert operations. The project's proposals included staging terrorist attacks and blaming them on Cuba, thereby creating a pretext for military intervention. This strategy of manufacturing false narratives and manipulating public opinion became a hallmark of unconventional warfare tactics in later years. The use of conspiracy theories as a tool to justify military actions has been observed in several instances throughout history, making Operation Northwoods a significant milestone in the evolution of such tactics.

Furthermore, the political ramifications and controversies surrounding Operation Northwoods cannot be ignored. The project revealed the extent to which government officials were willing to go in order to achieve their objectives, even if it meant sacrificing the truth and potentially endangering innocent lives. This created a climate of mistrust and skepticism among the public, leading to a heightened scrutiny of government actions and increased demands for transparency.

Another crucial aspect to explore is the role of the military-industrial complex in the planning of Operation Northwoods. The project was developed in close collaboration with defense contractors and other entities within the military-industrial complex. This highlights the influence of these powerful stakeholders in shaping military strategies and the potential for profit-driven motives to drive decision-making processes.

Comparisons between Operation Northwoods and other covert operations in U.S. history can also provide valuable insights. By examining similarities and differences, historians can gain a deeper understanding of the factors that contribute to the planning and execution of such operations, as well as their long-term consequences.

Lastly, the impact of Operation Northwoods on U.S.-Cuba relations and its legacy in shaping future military strategies should be analyzed. The project strained relations between the two countries and had a lasting impact on the geopolitical landscape of the region. Additionally, the tactics proposed in Operation Northwoods, such as psychological warfare and propaganda, continue to be utilized in contemporary conflicts, underscoring the enduring influence of this project on military strategies.

In conclusion, the analysis of Operation Northwoods provides historians with a rich and complex subject to explore. By examining its influence on the development of unconventional warfare tactics, its political ramifications, and its legacy in shaping future military strategies, a comprehensive understanding of this pivotal moment in history can be achieved.

Examination of the ethical considerations and moral boundaries of military strategies

In the subchapter "Examination of the ethical considerations and moral boundaries of military strategies," we delve into the profound ethical questions and moral dilemmas that arise when discussing military strategies. This thought-provoking analysis aims to shed light on the complex nature of Operation Northwoods and its wider implications for military interventions.

Throughout history, military strategies have sparked controversies and raised ethical concerns. Operation Northwoods, a covert project devised by the U.S. military in 1962 for military intervention in Cuba, serves as a prime case study to explore these considerations. This subchapter offers a comprehensive examination of the project's ethical dimensions.

Drawing upon historical analysis and extensive research, we dissect the decision-making process behind Operation Northwoods, scrutinizing the intricate interplay between government officials, military minds, and the military-industrial complex. By comparing it to other covert operations in U.S. history, we highlight the distinct features and potential long-lasting impact of Operation Northwoods.

The subchapter also delves into the political ramifications and controversies surrounding Operation Northwoods, addressing the conspiracy theories that have emerged in its wake. We explore the role of intelligence agencies in planning and executing such covert operations, providing valuable insights into the inner workings of these secretive organizations.

Furthermore, we examine the psychological warfare and propaganda tactics proposed in Operation Northwoods, revealing the extent to which moral boundaries were pushed in pursuit of political objectives. This analysis invites historians to reflect on the moral implications of manipulating public opinion and the psychological toll on both the perpetrators and the victims.

As we explore the declassification of Operation Northwoods documents, we consider the international response to this revelation. The subchapter investigates how these documents have shaped U.S.-Cuba relations and the broader legacy of Operation Northwoods in shaping future military strategies. By addressing the ethical considerations and moral boundaries of military strategies, we encourage historians to reflect on the lessons learned from Operation Northwoods and the need for robust ethical frameworks in military decision-making.

Overall, this subchapter provides a comprehensive examination of Operation Northwoods and its ethical implications. It invites historians to critically analyze the project's historical impact, its connection to conspiracy theories, and the pressing ethical questions it raises. By exploring the interplay between military strategies, political objectives, and moral boundaries, this analysis fosters a deeper understanding of the complex nature of military interventions and their lasting effects.

Lessons learned from Operation Northwoods and their integration into contemporary military doctrines

Title: Lessons Learned from Operation Northwoods and their Integration into Contemporary Military Doctrines

Introduction:

Operation Northwoods, the 1962 U.S. project for military intervention in Cuba, serves as a remarkable case study in understanding the complex dynamics of covert operations and their historical impact. This subchapter delves into the valuable lessons learned from Operation Northwoods and its integration into contemporary military doctrines. By examining the decision-making process, conspiracy theories, political ramifications, and the role of intelligence agencies, historians can gain a deeper understanding of this pivotal event.

Lesson 1: Historical Analysis of the Decision-Making Process

By dissecting the decision-making process behind Operation Northwoods, historians can uncover the intricate web of political, military, and intelligence influences that shaped the project. This analysis allows us to identify potential pitfalls and challenges in similar covert operations, enabling us to make better-informed decisions in the future.

Lesson 2: Comparisons with Other Covert Operations in U.S. History

Drawing comparisons between Operation Northwoods and other covert operations throughout U.S. history provides valuable insights into the evolution of military strategies. These comparisons shed light on the similarities and differences in tactics, objectives, and outcomes, enabling historians to identify recurring patterns and trends.

Lesson 3: Legacy of Operation Northwoods in Shaping Future Military Strategies

The legacy of Operation Northwoods extends beyond its immediate historical context. Understanding how this operation influenced subsequent military strategies allows for an examination of its lasting impact on national security policies. This analysis enables historians to identify the long-term ramifications of Operation Northwoods and its influence on contemporary military doctrines.

Lesson 4: Psychological Warfare and Propaganda Tactics Proposed in Operation Northwoods

Operation Northwoods proposed psychological warfare and propaganda tactics that were never implemented. By exploring these tactics, historians can gain insights into the mindset and strategies of the military-industrial complex during that era. This analysis also helps us assess the ethical implications of such tactics in modern warfare.

Lesson 5: International Response to the Declassification of Operation Northwoods Documents

The declassification of Operation Northwoods documents had a profound impact on international relations. Understanding the global response to the release of these documents allows historians to assess their significance in shaping public opinion, diplomatic relations, and perceptions of U.S. foreign policy.

Conclusion:

Lessons learned from Operation Northwoods have far-reaching implications for historians and military strategists alike. By examining the decision-making process, legacy, psychological warfare tactics, and international response, we gain a deeper understanding of covert operations, their historical impact, and their integration into contemporary military doctrines. This knowledge equips us with the insights necessary to navigate the complex world of covert operations and ensure a more informed and ethical approach to national security policies.

Chapter 9: Psychological warfare and propaganda tactics proposed in Operation Northwoods

Overview of the psychological warfare and propaganda strategies outlined in Operation Northwoods

Operation Northwoods, a highly controversial military project devised by the U.S. government in 1962, aimed to justify military intervention in Cuba through a series of covert tactics. This subchapter delves into the psychological warfare and propaganda strategies proposed in Operation Northwoods, shedding light on the intricate web of manipulation and misinformation that was intended to deceive both the American public and the international community.

At the core of Operation Northwoods were psychological warfare tactics designed to manipulate public opinion and create a justification for military action. The documents reveal plans to stage false flag attacks, such as hijacking civilian planes, attacking U.S. military ships, and orchestrating acts of terrorism on American soil. These staged events would be attributed to Cuban forces, painting them as a threat to national security and justifying military intervention.

Propaganda played a crucial role in Operation Northwoods, with plans to manipulate media outlets and disseminate false information to shape public perception. The documents outline strategies to plant false stories in the press, create fake Cuban radio broadcasts, and fabricate evidence to support the narrative of Cuban aggression. These tactics aimed to sway public opinion in favor of military action and garner support for the government's agenda.

The psychological warfare and propaganda strategies outlined in Operation Northwoods were not only intended to deceive the American public but also to manipulate international perception. By creating a false narrative of Cuban aggression, the U.S. government sought to rally international support for military intervention. The documents reveal plans to present fabricated evidence to foreign governments, manipulate international organizations, and use diplomatic channels to further their agenda.

The revelation of Operation Northwoods documents sparked intense political ramifications and controversies. It raised questions about the extent to which governments are willing to manipulate public opinion and the ethical boundaries of covert operations. The role of intelligence agencies in planning and executing such operations also came under scrutiny, leading to calls for greater transparency and accountability.

Operation Northwoods had a lasting impact on U.S.-Cuba relations, further straining an already tense relationship. The project's declassification exposed the extent of the U.S. government's hostility towards Cuba and its willingness to employ deceptive tactics. The legacy of Operation Northwoods also shaped future military strategies, prompting a reevaluation of the role of psychological warfare and propaganda in achieving political objectives.

Historians analyzing Operation Northwoods often draw comparisons with other covert operations in U.S. history, highlighting the similarities and differences in their strategies and objectives. The project's exposure shed light on the influence of the military-industrial complex in shaping government policies, fueling discussions about the blurred lines between defense and corporate interests.

The international response to the declassification of Operation Northwoods documents was met with shock and condemnation. It underscored the importance of transparency in government operations and fueled skepticism towards official narratives. The revelations of Operation Northwoods served as a cautionary tale, reminding the world of the dangers of unchecked power and the need for vigilance in questioning official narratives.

In conclusion, the psychological warfare and propaganda strategies proposed in Operation Northwoods were a shocking revelation of the lengths to which governments are willing to go to manipulate public opinion. The project's legacy continues to shape military strategies, fuel conspiracy theories, and provoke discussions about the role of intelligence agencies and the military-industrial complex. The international response to the declassification of Operation Northwoods documents serves as a reminder of the importance of transparency and accountability in government operations.

Analysis of the intended psychological impact on the Cuban population and international perception

Operation Northwoods was a highly controversial and covert military project proposed by the United States in 1962, aimed at justifying military intervention in Cuba. This subchapter delves into the intended psychological impact on the Cuban population and the subsequent international perception of these proposed actions.

The psychological impact on the Cuban population was a crucial aspect of Operation Northwoods. The project aimed to create fear and uncertainty within the Cuban people, thus destabilizing the government and provoking a popular uprising against Fidel Castro. Plans included orchestrating violent incidents, such as bombings and hijackings, which would be attributed to Cuban agents. These actions were designed to create an atmosphere of chaos and terror, leading to a loss of faith in the government's ability to protect its citizens.

Furthermore, the intended psychological impact extended beyond the Cuban population. Operation Northwoods aimed to manipulate international perception by portraying Cuba as a threat to regional and global security. By attributing these orchestrated incidents to the Cuban government, the United States sought to garner international support for military intervention in Cuba. The project recognized the importance of shaping public opinion and generating a narrative that justified American military action.

The ramifications of such psychological warfare and propaganda tactics proposed in Operation Northwoods are significant. This subchapter explores the potential consequences of these actions, including the erosion of trust in government institutions, the manipulation of public opinion, and the potential for escalation of conflict. It also examines the lasting impact of Operation Northwoods on U.S.-Cuba relations, including the erosion of trust between the two nations and the perpetuation of conspiracy theories surrounding covert operations.

Moreover, this subchapter highlights the role of intelligence agencies in planning and executing covert operations like Operation Northwoods. It examines the decision-making process behind the project, shedding light on the political motivations and pressures that influenced its development. Comparisons are drawn between Operation Northwoods and other covert operations in U.S. history, providing historical context and insight into the broader implications of such actions.

Finally, this subchapter addresses the international response to the declassification of Operation Northwoods documents. Historians and scholars have scrutinized these documents, seeking to understand the true extent of the proposed actions and their potential impact on global affairs. The declassification has sparked debates surrounding the ethics and legality of covert operations, as well as the role of the military-industrial complex in shaping military strategies.

In conclusion, the analysis of the intended psychological impact on the Cuban population and international perception in Operation Northwoods is crucial to understanding the historical impact of this covert military project. By examining the motivations, tactics, and consequences of these proposed actions, historians can shed light on the intricate dynamics between nations and the lasting legacy of such operations on global affairs.

Ethical implications of psychological warfare and propaganda in military operations

Psychological warfare and propaganda have long been tools utilized by military forces in order to gain an advantage over their adversaries. However, the ethical implications of these tactics are complex and often controversial. In the context of military operations, the use of psychological warfare and propaganda raises questions about the boundaries of acceptable conduct, the manipulation of information, and the impact on civilian populations.

One notable case that highlights these ethical concerns is Operation Northwoods, a secret project developed by the U.S. military in 1962 to justify military intervention in Cuba. While the operation was never implemented, its existence and the proposed tactics it involved shed light on the moral dilemmas faced by military decision-makers.

The proposed strategies in Operation Northwoods included false flag attacks, staged incidents, and the dissemination of fabricated information to manipulate public opinion. These tactics aimed to create a pretext for military action, but they also reveal the potential for abuse of power and the manipulation of public sentiment.

From a historical perspective, analyzing the decision-making process behind Operation Northwoods provides insights into the political ramifications and controversies surrounding the operation. It raises questions about the role of the military-industrial complex in shaping military strategies and the extent to which covert operations are driven by political agendas.

Comparisons between Operation Northwoods and other covert operations in U.S. history further highlight the recurrent theme of ethical implications. This prompts historians to consider the broader impact of such operations on international relations, particularly in the case of U.S.-Cuba relations.

The legacy of Operation Northwoods also plays a crucial role in shaping future military strategies. It serves as a cautionary tale, emphasizing the need for transparency, accountability, and adherence to ethical principles in military planning.

Furthermore, the psychological warfare and propaganda tactics proposed in Operation Northwoods raise concerns about the role of intelligence agencies in planning and executing covert operations. Historians must critically examine the ethical boundaries within which these agencies operate, and the impact of their actions on global perceptions of the countries they represent.

Lastly, the international response to the declassification of Operation Northwoods documents highlights the significance of public awareness and scrutiny in holding governments accountable for their actions. It underscores the importance of maintaining a vigilant and informed society that questions the ethical implications of military operations.

In conclusion, the ethical implications of psychological warfare and propaganda in military operations, as exemplified by Operation Northwoods, raise profound questions about the moral boundaries of warfare, the manipulation of information, and the impact on civilian populations. Historians play a crucial role in analyzing and critiquing these implications, ensuring that ethical considerations remain at the forefront of military decision-making in the future.

Lessons learned from Operation Northwoods for the future use of psychological warfare

Title: Lessons Learned from Operation Northwoods for the Future Use of Psychological Warfare

Introduction:

Operation Northwoods, the infamous 1962 U.S. project for military intervention in Cuba, serves as a pivotal point in history that raises several important questions about the use of psychological warfare. This subchapter aims to explore the valuable lessons that can be derived from Operation Northwoods and their implications for future military strategies. Addressed to historians, this chapter delves into the intricate details of this covert operation, shedding light on its historical impact, political ramifications, and controversies. Moreover, it examines the decision-making process, the role of the military-industrial complex, and the comparisons with other covert operations in U.S. history. It also analyzes the impact on U.S.-Cuba relations, the legacy it left, and the psychological warfare and propaganda tactics proposed during the operation. Lastly, this subchapter delves into the role of intelligence agencies and the international response to the declassification of Operation Northwoods documents.

Lessons Learned:

Operation Northwoods provides invaluable lessons that can shape future military strategies and shed light on the risks associated with psychological warfare. Firstly, it highlights the potential dangers of unchecked power within intelligence agencies and the military-industrial complex, emphasizing the need for robust oversight and transparency. The decision-making process behind Operation Northwoods exposed the vulnerability of democratic systems to manipulation by influential entities.

Secondly, the operation underscores the importance of critically analyzing the political ramifications and controversies surrounding covert operations. It serves as a reminder of the potential consequences of pursuing questionable agendas, both domestically and internationally. Historical analysis reveals the extent to which Operation Northwoods strained U.S.-Cuba relations, leading to enduring mistrust and hostility.

Furthermore, Operation Northwoods offers insight into the effectiveness of psychological warfare and propaganda tactics. The proposed strategies during this operation demonstrate the ability to manipulate public opinion and shape narratives to justify military intervention. Understanding these tactics is crucial for recognizing and countering their implementation in future conflicts.

Conclusion:

In conclusion, Operation Northwoods is a pivotal event in U.S. history that holds significant lessons for the future use of psychological warfare. Historians and researchers must analyze the political, historical, and ethical dimensions of this operation to gain a comprehensive understanding of its implications. By learning from the past, we can develop strategies and policies that prioritize transparency, accountability, and the ethical use of psychological warfare. The declassification of Operation Northwoods documents and the international response to them highlight the importance of open dialogue and the need for a global understanding of the potential consequences of covert operations. Ultimately, these lessons can guide us towards a more responsible and informed approach to psychological warfare, ensuring that history does not repeat itself.

Chapter 10: The role of intelligence agencies in planning and executing covert operations like Operation Northwoods

Examination of the involvement of intelligence agencies in the planning of Operation Northwoods

Operation Northwoods, the infamous 1962 U.S. project for military intervention in Cuba, has long been a subject of fascination and controversy. As historians delve into the details of this covert operation, one aspect that demands careful examination is the role of intelligence agencies in its planning. The involvement of these agencies, particularly the Central Intelligence Agency (CIA), raises significant questions about the decision-making process and the extent to which covert operations are executed.

To fully understand the intelligence agencies' involvement in Operation Northwoods, it is crucial to explore the historical context surrounding the project. The book "Operation Northwoods and U.S.-Cuba Relations: A Historical Impact" meticulously analyzes the political ramifications and controversies that shaped the operation. Moreover, it provides a comprehensive historical analysis of the decision-making process behind Operation Northwoods, shedding light on the various factors that influenced its planning.

Comparisons between Operation Northwoods and other covert operations in U.S. history offer valuable insights into the intelligence agencies' modus operandi. By examining similar operations, such as the Bay of Pigs invasion or the Iran-Contra affair, historians can identify patterns and recurring themes in the planning and execution of covert operations. Such comparisons allow for a deeper understanding of the intelligence agencies' role in shaping future military strategies.

The book also explores the psychological warfare and propaganda tactics proposed in Operation Northwoods. These tactics, ranging from false flag operations to staged acts of terrorism, reveal the extent to which intelligence agencies were willing to manipulate public opinion to achieve their objectives. By examining these tactics, historians gain a better understanding of the lengths to which intelligence agencies are ready to go to achieve their goals.

Furthermore, the international response to the declassification of Operation Northwoods documents is an important aspect to consider. The revelation of this covert operation had far-reaching implications for U.S.-Cuba relations and the global perception of American foreign policy. Understanding the international response to these declassified documents provides historians with a broader perspective on the legacy of Operation Northwoods.

In conclusion, the examination of the involvement of intelligence agencies in the planning of Operation Northwoods is a crucial component of understanding this historical event. By exploring the decision-making process, comparing it to other covert operations, and analyzing the psychological warfare tactics proposed, historians can shed light on the complex web of intrigue surrounding Operation Northwoods. Furthermore, understanding the international response to the declassification of Operation Northwoods documents allows for a comprehensive assessment of its historical impact.

Analysis of the intelligence-gathering process and its impact on decision-making

In this subchapter, we delve into the intricate details of the intelligence-gathering process and its profound impact on decision-making. By examining the historical context of Operation Northwoods, we shed light on the complex dynamics that shaped the decision-making process behind this infamous project. Targeted towards historians and those interested in Operation Northwoods, this analysis aims to provide a comprehensive understanding of the various facets surrounding this controversial operation.

Firstly, we explore the conspiracy theories that have arisen around Operation Northwoods. By critically examining the evidence and historical records, we aim to separate fact from fiction and shed light on the truth behind this covert operation. Furthermore, we delve into the political ramifications and controversies that surrounded Operation Northwoods, focusing on the implications it had on U.S.-Cuba relations.

One crucial aspect we address is the role of the military-industrial complex in planning Operation Northwoods. By analyzing the influence of defense contractors and their vested interests, we aim to uncover the motivations behind this project and its implications for future military strategies.

Drawing comparisons between Operation Northwoods and other covert operations in U.S. history, we provide a broader historical analysis. This approach allows us to discern patterns and understand the broader implications of such operations on national security and international relations.

Moreover, we examine the psychological warfare and propaganda tactics proposed in Operation Northwoods. By exploring the intelligence agencies' involvement in planning and executing such covert operations, we shed light on the mechanisms underlying their decision-making processes.

The declassification of Operation Northwoods documents triggered an international response, which we analyze in detail. We explore the impact of this revelation on U.S.-Cuba relations and its broader implications for international diplomacy.

Lastly, we investigate the legacy of Operation Northwoods in shaping future military strategies. By understanding the historical impact of this operation, we gain insights into the evolution of intelligence-gathering techniques and their influence on decision-making.

Through this subchapter, historians and those interested in Operation Northwoods will gain a comprehensive understanding of the intelligence-gathering process and its far-reaching effects on decision-making. By examining the historical context, political ramifications, and international response, we aim to shed light on the intricacies surrounding this controversial operation and its implications for U.S.-Cuba relations and future military strategies.

Discussion of the relationship between intelligence agencies and political leadership

The relationship between intelligence agencies and political leadership has long been a subject of scrutiny and debate. In the context of Operation Northwoods and its impact on U.S.-Cuba relations, this relationship becomes even more crucial to examine. This subchapter aims to delve into the intricate dynamics between intelligence agencies and political leadership, shedding light on the decision-making process, controversies, and ramifications of Operation Northwoods.

Intelligence agencies, such as the CIA and the Pentagon, play a pivotal role in shaping national security policies and strategies. Their expertise in gathering and analyzing intelligence is essential for political leaders to make informed decisions. However, the extent to which intelligence agencies influence political leadership and vice versa is a delicate balance that can sometimes be compromised.

Operation Northwoods, a covert plan proposed in 1962 for military intervention in Cuba, serves as a prime example of this complex relationship. The historical analysis of the decision-making process behind Operation Northwoods reveals the intricate web of interests, motivations, and pressures that influenced both the intelligence agencies and the political leadership.

One of the key aspects to consider is the role of the military-industrial complex in planning Operation Northwoods. The military-industrial complex, comprising defense contractors and the armed forces, has a vested interest in promoting military interventions and maintaining a state of perpetual warfare. The influence of this complex on intelligence agencies and political leadership cannot be overlooked when examining Operation Northwoods.

Comparisons between Operation Northwoods and other covert operations in U.S. history shed light on the broader patterns and strategies employed by intelligence agencies. The psychological warfare and propaganda tactics proposed in Operation Northwoods reveal the lengths to which intelligence agencies are willing to go in manipulating public opinion and justifying military interventions.

Furthermore, the impact of Operation Northwoods on U.S.-Cuba relations cannot be underestimated. The declassification of Operation Northwoods documents led to an international response, with many countries expressing shock and concern over the proposed actions. This response highlights the significance of intelligence agencies' actions and their potential consequences on diplomatic relations.

In conclusion, the relationship between intelligence agencies and political leadership is complex and multifaceted. Operation Northwoods serves as a case study to explore the intricate dynamics between these entities. By analyzing the decision-making process, controversies, and ramifications of Operation Northwoods, historians can gain a deeper understanding of the role intelligence agencies play in shaping military strategies, the impact on international relations, and the broader implications for future covert operations.

Implications for the oversight and accountability of intelligence operations

The subchapter "Implications for the Oversight and Accountability of Intelligence Operations" delves into the far-reaching consequences of Operation Northwoods, shedding light on the need for robust mechanisms to monitor and regulate intelligence activities. Historians and those interested in Operation Northwoods will find this section particularly insightful as it explores the broader implications of this covert operation.

One of the key areas of focus is the political ramifications and controversies surrounding Operation Northwoods. The chapter examines how the project, which aimed to stage false flag attacks as pretexts for military intervention in Cuba, raised significant ethical and legal concerns. It highlights the importance of understanding the decision-making process behind Operation Northwoods to grasp the complex dynamics within the U.S. government during the early 1960s.

Moreover, the subchapter explores the role of the military-industrial complex in planning Operation Northwoods. By analyzing the interplay between defense contractors, the military, and political actors, historians gain valuable insights into the influence wielded by these entities in shaping military strategies and covert operations.

Drawing comparisons between Operation Northwoods and other covert operations in U.S. history, the chapter provides a historical analysis of the decision-making processes behind such operations. This comparative approach allows historians to contextualize Operation Northwoods within a broader framework, enhancing their understanding of the historical significance of this covert operation.

Furthermore, the subchapter delves into the impact of Operation Northwoods on U.S.-Cuba relations. By examining the declassified documents related to this operation, historians can uncover the long-lasting implications it had on diplomatic ties and regional dynamics. This analysis also sheds light on the legacy of Operation Northwoods in shaping future military strategies, both within the United States and globally.

The subchapter also explores the psychological warfare and propaganda tactics proposed in Operation Northwoods. By examining these proposed methods, historians gain a deeper understanding of the strategies employed by intelligence agencies during this time, underscoring the importance of oversight and accountability in intelligence operations.

Lastly, the subchapter touches upon the international response to the declassification of Operation Northwoods documents. By analyzing how this revelation was received globally, historians can assess the broader implications of covert operations on international relations and public perception.

Overall, this subchapter offers historians a comprehensive exploration of the implications for the oversight and accountability of intelligence operations, drawing on the specific case of Operation Northwoods. By delving into the political, historical, and ethical dimensions of this covert operation, it provides a rich and nuanced understanding of the broader implications for intelligence activities.

Chapter 11: The international response to the declassification of Operation Northwoods documents

Reactions and opinions from foreign governments and international organizations

The declassification of Operation Northwoods documents sent shockwaves throughout the international community, eliciting a range of reactions and opinions from foreign governments and international organizations. Historians have delved into the aftermath of this revelation, highlighting the significance of these responses in shaping the perception of the United States and its covert operations.

Many foreign governments expressed their deep concern and condemnation of Operation Northwoods. Diplomatic cables and official statements from countries such as the Soviet Union, China, and various Latin American nations revealed a sense of outrage and betrayal. These governments saw the project as a blatant violation of international law, an affront to the principles of sovereignty, and a dangerous precedent for future military interventions. The revelations of Operation Northwoods also fueled existing suspicions and conspiracy theories surrounding U.S. intentions in Latin America and beyond.

International organizations, including the United Nations and the Organization of American States, were quick to denounce Operation Northwoods as a grave threat to regional and global stability. Calls for an immediate investigation into the project and demands for the United States to be held accountable resonated within these forums. It became evident that Operation Northwoods had not only damaged U.S.-Cuba relations but also strained the country's credibility on the global stage.

The fallout from Operation Northwoods had far-reaching political ramifications. It exposed the darker side of U.S. foreign policy and cast doubt on the integrity of decision-making processes within the government. Historians have analyzed the impact of these revelations on public opinion, both domestically and internationally. The project's exposure further fueled anti-American sentiment in Cuba and strengthened the resolve of other nations to guard against potential U.S. aggression.

Operation Northwoods also highlighted the role of the military-industrial complex in shaping covert operations and military strategies. The project's proposals for psychological warfare and propaganda tactics underscored the significant influence of defense contractors and the intelligence community in planning and executing such operations. Comparisons with other covert operations in U.S. history shed light on the broader patterns and practices employed by the government in pursuing its geopolitical objectives.

The declassification of Operation Northwoods documents not only provided historians with valuable insights into a specific historical event but also sparked a broader conversation about the legacy of covert operations and the role of intelligence agencies. The international response to these revelations played a crucial role in shaping future military strategies and influencing the way intelligence agencies operate.

In conclusion, the reactions and opinions from foreign governments and international organizations to the declassification of Operation Northwoods documents were significant in understanding the historical impact of this covert project. They not only showcased the international condemnation of the United States' actions but also shed light on the broader implications for U.S.-Cuba relations, political controversies, and the role of intelligence agencies in shaping military strategies. By examining these responses, historians gain a deeper understanding of the complexities and consequences of Operation Northwoods and its lasting effects on global politics.

Examination of the impact on global perceptions of U.S. foreign policy and military intentions

The subchapter titled "Examination of the Impact on Global Perceptions of U.S. Foreign Policy and Military Intentions" explores the far-reaching consequences of Operation Northwoods and its implications for U.S. foreign policy and military intentions. This section delves into the historical impact of the covert operation, shedding light on its significance for historians and various niche audiences.

Operation Northwoods, the infamous 1962 U.S. project for military intervention in Cuba, never implemented but nevertheless left a lasting imprint on global perceptions of U.S. foreign policy. This section delves into the conspiracy theories surrounding Operation Northwoods, examining the controversies and political ramifications associated with this secret plan. By analyzing the decision-making process behind Operation Northwoods, historians gain valuable insights into the historical context and the factors that shaped U.S. military strategies during the Cold War.

Furthermore, this subchapter explores the role of the military-industrial complex in planning Operation Northwoods. By examining comparisons between Operation Northwoods and other covert operations in U.S. history, historians can discern patterns and trends in the implementation of such operations, shedding light on the broader strategies employed by the U.S. government.

The impact of Operation Northwoods on U.S.-Cuba relations is another crucial aspect explored in this subchapter. By analyzing the declassified documents and historical records, historians can evaluate the legacy of Operation Northwoods in shaping future military strategies, both in relation to Cuba and beyond. Moreover, this section delves into the psychological warfare and propaganda tactics proposed in Operation Northwoods, providing a deeper understanding of the strategies employed by intelligence agencies in planning and executing covert operations.

Lastly, this subchapter examines the international response to the declassification of Operation Northwoods documents. By exploring how this revelation influenced global perceptions of U.S. foreign policy and military intentions, historians gain valuable insights into the diplomatic fallout and long-term implications of Operation Northwoods.

Overall, this subchapter delves into the multifaceted aspects surrounding Operation Northwoods, offering historians and niche audiences a comprehensive analysis of its historical impact, political ramifications, and the broader implications for U.S. foreign policy and military intentions.

Analysis of the international legal implications of Operation Northwoods

In this subchapter, we delve into the international legal implications of Operation Northwoods, a covert project that had far-reaching consequences on U.S.-Cuba relations. Historians and those interested in the intricacies of Operation Northwoods will find this analysis enlightening, as it explores the legal dimensions of this controversial operation.

Operation Northwoods, the 1962 U.S. project for military intervention in Cuba that was never implemented, was surrounded by conspiracy theories and political ramifications. However, it is crucial to understand the historical impact of the decision-making process behind this operation, especially from a legal perspective.

One key aspect to explore is the role of the military-industrial complex in planning Operation Northwoods. By examining the involvement of defense contractors and their influence on the decision-making process, we can gain insights into the complex dynamics of military strategies during that era.

Comparisons between Operation Northwoods and other covert operations in U.S. history also shed light on the legal implications. Understanding how these operations were executed and the legal boundaries they pushed helps us contextualize the significance of Operation Northwoods in shaping future military strategies.

Moreover, Operation Northwoods proposed psychological warfare and propaganda tactics, leading to questions about the legality of such methods. Analyzing the legal aspects of these tactics provides a deeper understanding of the ethical and legal dilemmas posed by covert operations.

Intelligence agencies played a crucial role in planning and executing Operation Northwoods, raising issues regarding their accountability and the legal framework under which they operated. By examining the legal constraints (or lack thereof) on intelligence agencies during this period, we can gain valuable insights into the functioning of covert operations.

Additionally, we explore the international response to the declassification of Operation Northwoods documents. This response, both from Cuba and other nations, provides an understanding of the global perception of U.S. actions and the legal implications that arise when such covert operations come to light.

Overall, this subchapter offers a comprehensive analysis of the international legal implications of Operation Northwoods. By examining the historical impact, political ramifications, and legal dimensions of this operation, we gain a deeper understanding of its significance in shaping U.S.-Cuba relations and the broader landscape of covert operations. Historians and those interested in the intricate details of Operation Northwoods will find this analysis invaluable in unraveling the legal complexities of this controversial operation.

Lessons learned from the international response to Operation Northwoods and their influence on future covert operations.

Lessons learned from the international response to Operation Northwoods and their influence on future covert operations

Operation Northwoods has remained a significant event in U.S.-Cuba relations, sparking conspiracy theories and igniting political controversies. As historians delve into the historical impact of this covert operation, it becomes evident that the international response to its declassification has yielded valuable lessons that continue to shape future covert operations.

One of the key lessons learned from the international response to Operation Northwoods is the importance of transparency in decision-making processes. The declassification of Operation Northwoods documents shed light on the decision-making process behind this covert operation, revealing the intricate involvement of intelligence agencies and the military-industrial complex. Historians can analyze this historical episode to understand the complexities and challenges associated with covert operations, ultimately advocating for transparency and accountability in contemporary military strategies.

Furthermore, the international response to Operation Northwoods underscored the significance of maintaining ethical standards in covert operations. The proposed psychological warfare and propaganda tactics raised ethical concerns among the international community. Historians can examine this aspect of Operation Northwoods to explore the ethical boundaries and dilemmas faced by intelligence agencies, emphasizing the need for ethical frameworks to guide future covert operations.

The impact of Operation Northwoods on U.S.-Cuba relations cannot be understated. The international response to the declassification of Operation Northwoods documents revealed the extent of U.S. plans for military intervention in Cuba. This revelation strained diplomatic ties and fueled mistrust between the two nations. Historians can analyze the consequences of Operation Northwoods on U.S.-Cuba relations to gain insights into the long-lasting effects of covert operations on international diplomacy.

Operation Northwoods also highlighted the power dynamics between intelligence agencies and political leaders. The historical analysis of the decision-making process behind Operation Northwoods provides valuable insights into the influence of intelligence agencies on covert operations. Understanding this dynamic is crucial for historians and policymakers alike in order to prevent the abuse of power and ensure democratic oversight in future covert operations.

In conclusion, the international response to Operation Northwoods offers valuable lessons for historians and sheds light on the intricacies of covert operations. From the importance of transparency and ethical considerations to the impact on international relations and power dynamics, Operation Northwoods provides a comprehensive case study for understanding the complexities of covert operations. By learning from the past, historians can contribute to the development of more responsible and accountable strategies in the future.